Follow the Prophet

By SHAUNA GIBBY

Illustrated by BRYAN BEACH

DESERET
BOOK

Salt Lake City, Utah

© 2019 Shauna N. Gibby

Illustrations © 2019 Bryan Beach DBA Beachouse Multimedia

Visit us at deseretbook.com

Library of Congress Cataloging-in-Publication Data

Names: Gibby, Shauna, author.
Title: Follow the prophet : a flashlight discovery book / Shauna Gibby.
Description: Salt Lake City, Utah : Deseret Book, [2019]
Identifiers: LCCN 2018047213 | ISBN 9781629725765 (hardbound : alk. paper)
Subjects: LCSH: Prophets (Mormon theology)—Juvenile literature. | Mormon children—Conduct of life—Juvenile literature. | Mormon children—Religious life—Juvenile literature. | The Church of Jesus Christ of Latter-day Saints—History—Juvenile literature. | Picture books for children. | LCGFT: Picture books.
Classification: LCC BX8643.P7 G53 2019 | DDC 289.3092/2—dc23
LC record available at https://lccn.loc.gov/2018047213

Printed in China
RR Donnelley, Shenzhen, Guangdong, China   1/2019

10 9 8 7 6 5 4 3 2 1

To Larene, LouCeil, and Margie.
Thank you for being a guiding influence in my life.

—SG

To Pam, Milli, Liam, Greta, Phoebe, Hazel, and Aggi.

—BB

The prophet is a person who has been called by God to speak for Him and lead His Church on earth. There were prophets in Bible and Book of Mormon times and there are prophets today. When you look closely at each page, you will learn about some of the prophets and how they help us learn God's will.

Shine a flashlight behind the color pages to see what is hidden in each scene.

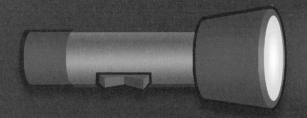

This is Adam and his wife, Eve.
They were the first people on Earth.
They lived in a beautiful garden
with many good things to eat.

Who came and visited Adam
in the garden?

Heavenly Father and Jesus
visited Adam and Eve and taught them what was right. After Adam and Eve left the garden, Adam taught his children and grandchildren the things that he learned from God. Adam was the first prophet.

This is Moses. He led a large group of people out of Egypt so they didn't have to be slaves anymore. Moses went to a mountain to talk with God and find out what the people should do.

What did God give him?

The Lord wrote ten commandments
on stone tablets and gave them to Moses. The
commandments taught Moses's people what is
right and wrong so they could be safe and happy.
The commandments still help guide us today.

Elijah was a prophet. He told the king and queen that they must repent or there would be no water or food in the land. The queen was angry and wanted to kill Elijah. He hid in the wilderness and the famine came.

How did he get food?

God sent birds to bring food to Elijah.
Later, he stayed with a woman and her
son. Elijah blessed their food so it lasted
a very long time. It was a miracle.

Malachi was another prophet in the Old Testament. He taught people that Jesus would come to live on the earth and that they should pay tithing. He also saw something that would happen in our time.

What was it?

He taught that children would seek to learn
about their ancestors and that families
would be united through temple work.
We now call this family history.

Lehi was a prophet in the Book of Mormon. He was warned by the Lord to take his family away from Jerusalem. They lived in tents in the wilderness. One morning, Lehi found something unusual outside his tent.

Do you know what it was?

It was a director or compass called the
Liahona. It was a ball that was very helpful
to Lehi's family. It was a gift from God that
had two pointers and gave directions. When
they were obedient, it showed them the way
to go as they traveled in the wilderness.

Mosiah's people, the Nephites, had been at war with the Lamanites for a long time. The Lord told Mosiah they needed to find a new place to live.

Where did the Lord lead Mosiah and his people?

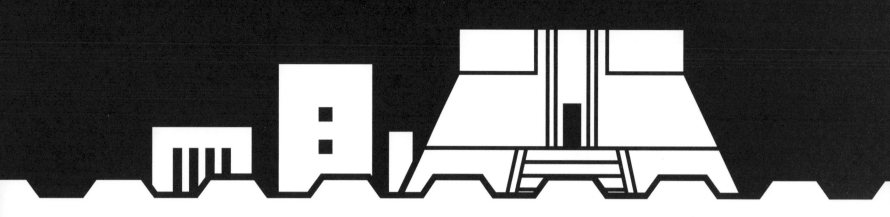

As they traveled through the wilderness,
Mosiah and his people discovered a city called
Zarahemla. The people there did not have any
scriptures, so they were happy to have a prophet
who had the scriptures and could teach them.

Nephi, the grandson of Helaman, was the prophet after Samuel the Lamanite taught the people that Jesus Christ would soon be born. The wicked people said they would kill those who believed in Christ if the signs of His birth didn't happen soon. Nephi prayed for his people.

What happened then?

The Lord told Nephi not to worry because
Jesus Christ would be born the next day.
A new star appeared in the sky, just as the
prophets said it would. Many people believed
the sign, repented, and were baptized.

This is John. He was Jesus Christ's friend and a prophet. He lived in the wilderness and many people came to hear him teach the gospel.

What did they call him?

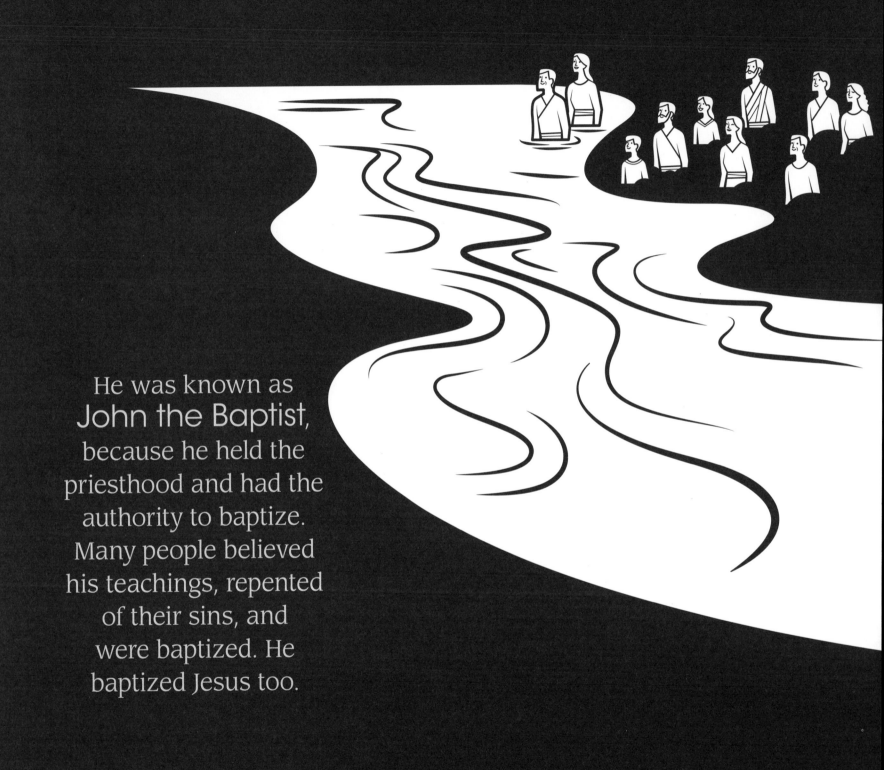

He was known as
John the Baptist,
because he held the
priesthood and had the
authority to baptize.
Many people believed
his teachings, repented
of their sins, and
were baptized. He
baptized Jesus too.

Peter was one of Jesus's apostles. Jesus told his apostles that Peter would be the leader of the Church on the earth after Jesus died. He told Peter he would give him something.

What was it?

Jesus gave Peter the keys of the kingdom. He meant that Peter had the priesthood and the power from God to guide and direct the Church. We often show Peter holding keys as a symbol of this authority. With the priesthood, Peter was able to do many things, like healing the sick, just as Jesus had done.

After all of Jesus's apostles died, His Church was no longer on the earth. Many years later, Heavenly Father and Jesus Christ appeared to a young man named Joseph Smith. Joseph was guided to something very important buried in a hill in the state of New York.

Who showed him where to go?

An angel named Moroni showed Joseph where to find the golden plates. With God's help, Joseph translated the writing on the plates into English. This translation became the Book of Mormon. He became the first latter-day prophet and restored the Church on the earth.

Lorenzo Snow was another latter-day prophet. While he was the prophet, the Church owed money to many people. One year there was not enough rain for the crops to grow.

What did President Snow tell the people of the Church?

He told them to pay their tithing. The Lord told him that this would bless the people and their crops. When the people paid their tithing, the crops grew and the Church had enough money to pay its debts.

David O. McKay was the prophet about 120 years after the Church had been restored.

What did the Lord have President McKay do to help the Church grow?

President McKay talked about how important
missionary work is. He created lessons for
the missionaries to teach, and had a school built
for them to learn foreign languages. He also said
that *every* member should be a missionary and
teach the gospel to those around them.

Gordon B. Hinckley was the prophet
after many people had joined the Church.
These members lived all over the world.

What did President Hinckley
do to bless the people?

He followed the Lord's direction to build many
temples all over the world. Many Church members
lived too far away to come to the temples, so
President Hinckley had more than 100 new temples
built. Now lots of people can go to the temple so
they can be together with their families forever.

We now have a prophet who helps us know what we should do. Heavenly Father teaches him what is right and then he teaches us.

How can we hear his words?

We can **hear** the words of President Russell M. Nelson at general conference, **read** what he says in Church magazines, and **listen** to our teachers and parents, who help us learn about him.

We are very blessed to have the words of prophets from the scriptures and have living prophets to guide us. They give us direction in a confusing world so we know what is right.